MW01071016

WOLF
COLORING BOOK

AN ADULT COLORING BOOK OF WOLVES FEATURING 40 WOLF DESIGNS IN VARIOUS STYLES

ADULT COLORING WORLD

ISBN-13: 978-1519574800

ISBN-10: 1519574800

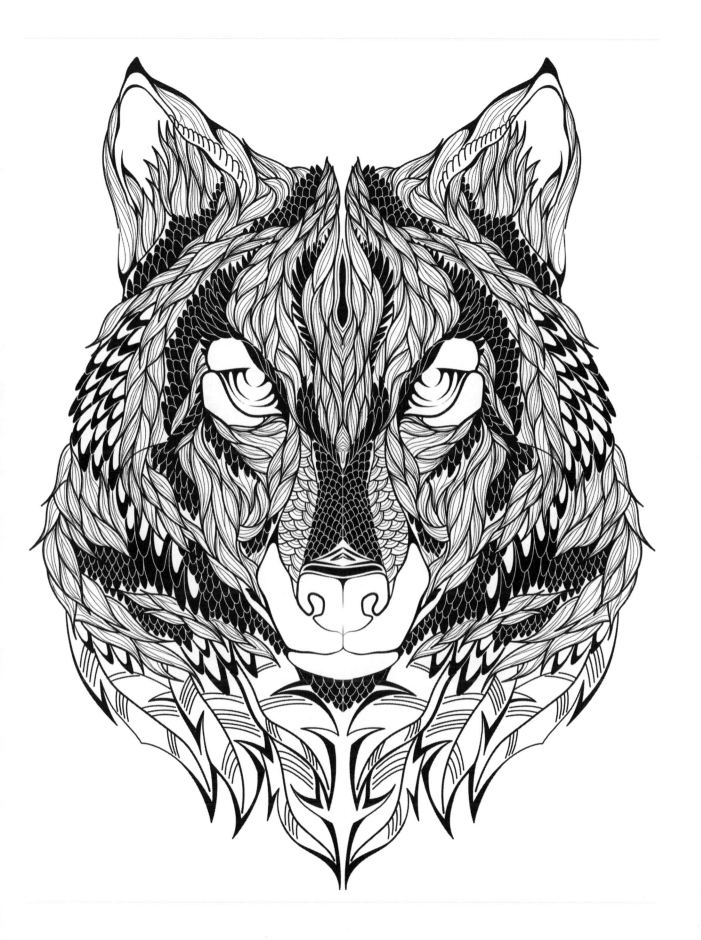

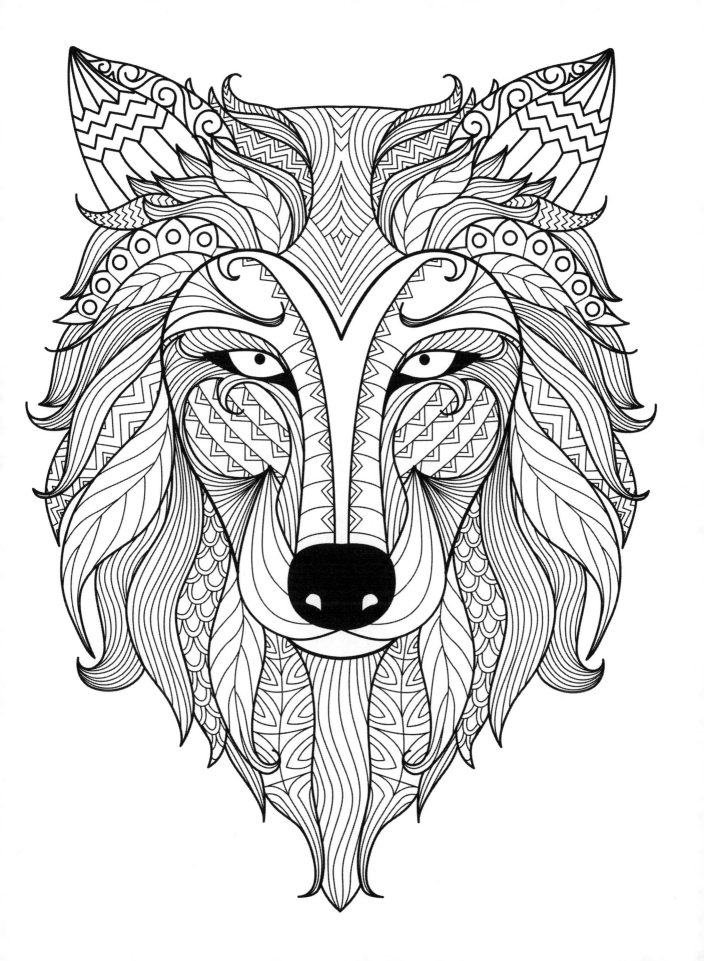

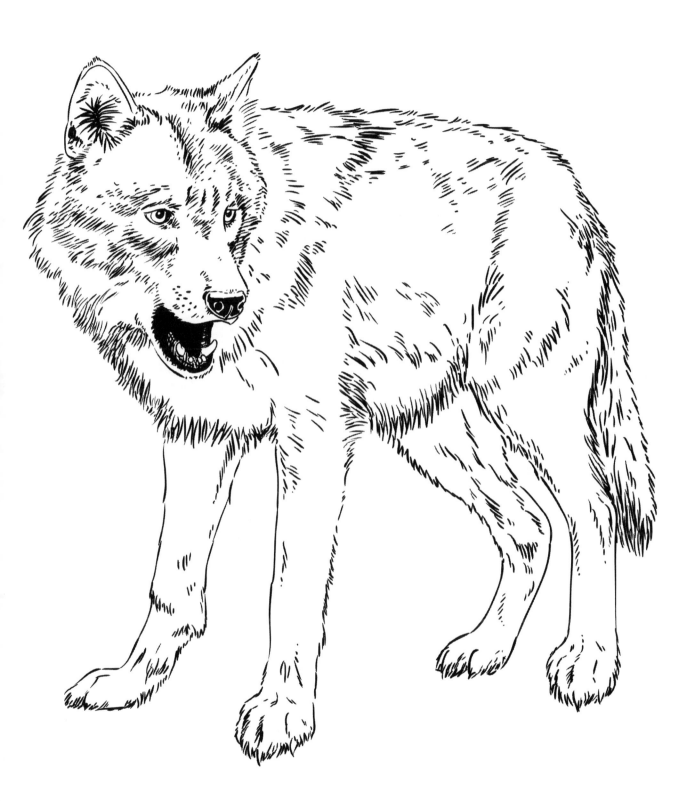

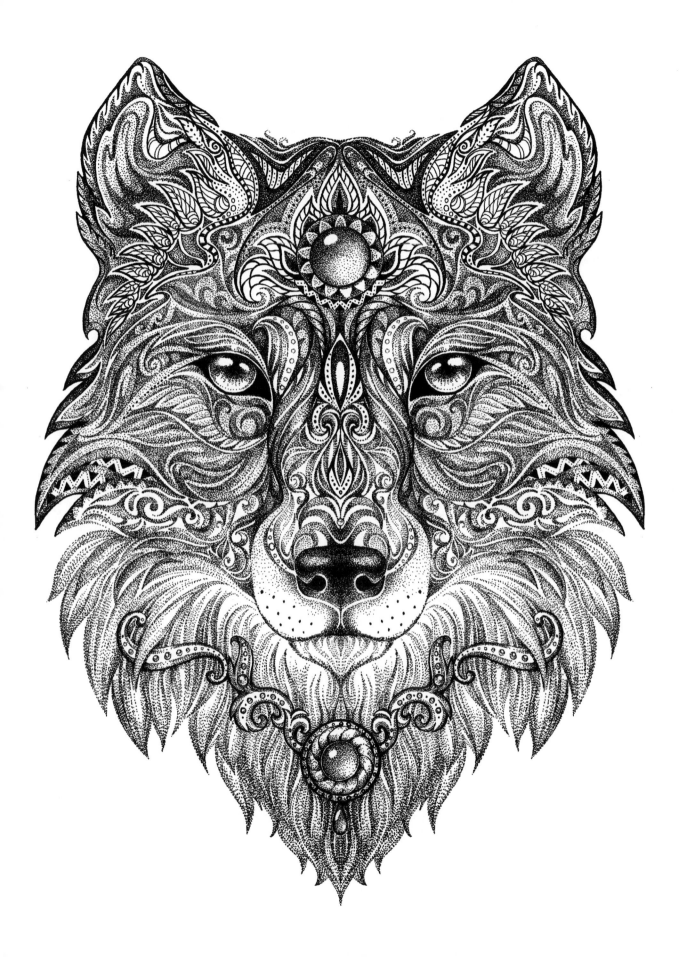

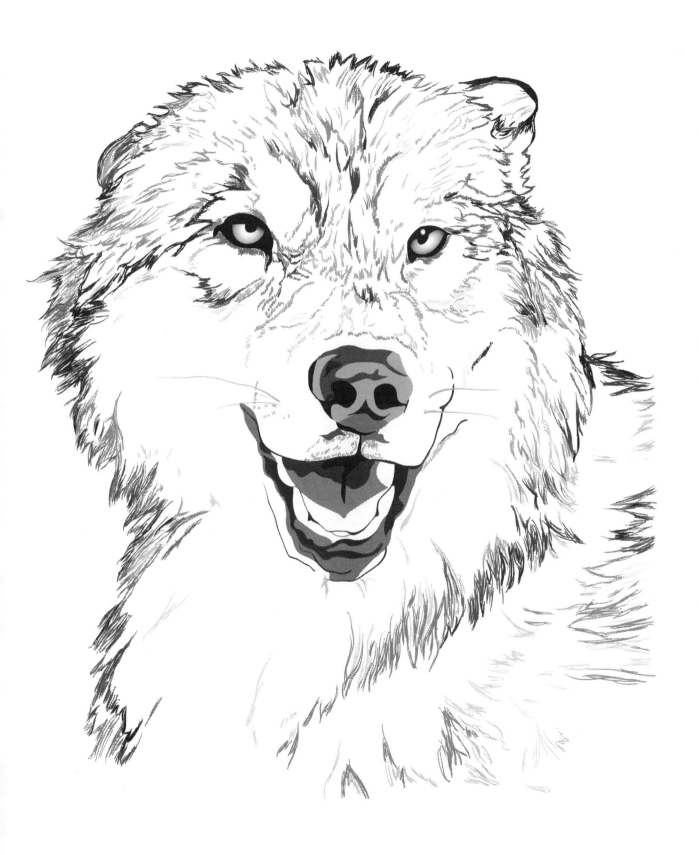

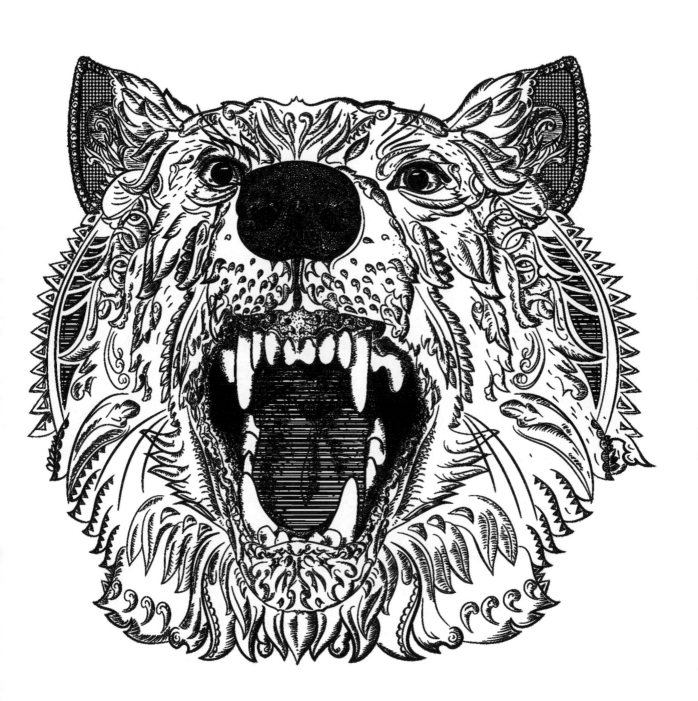

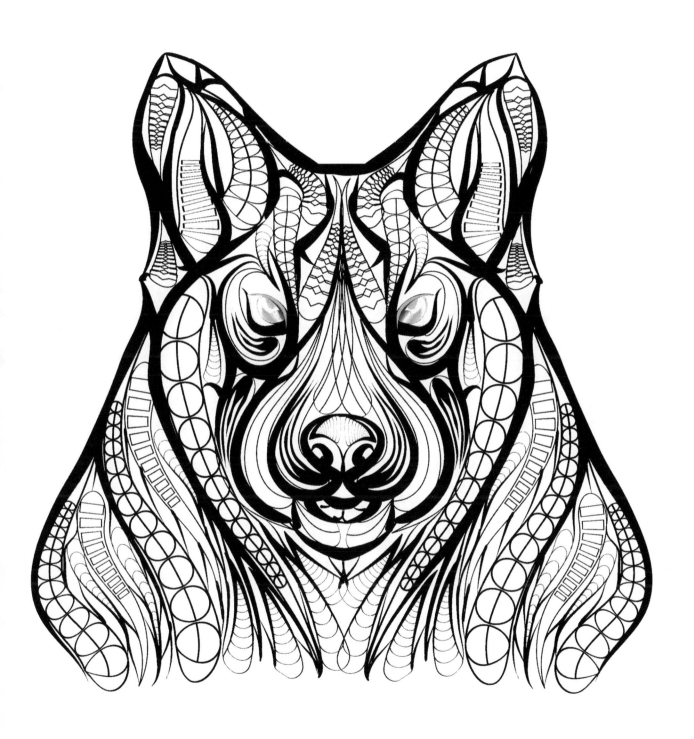

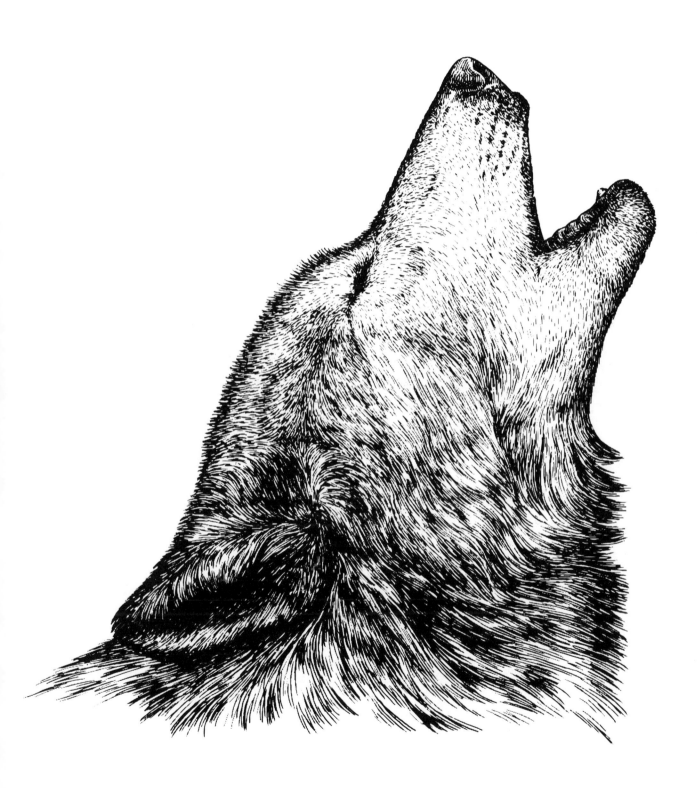

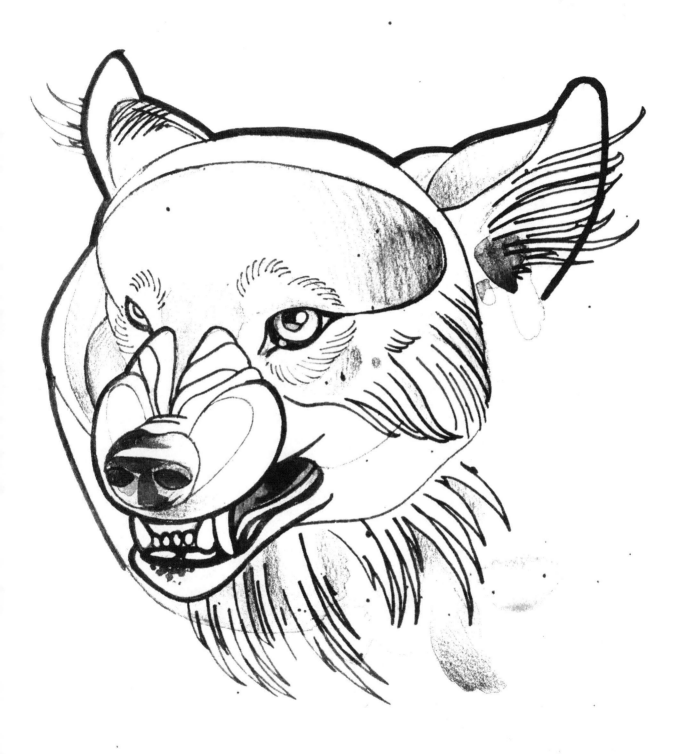

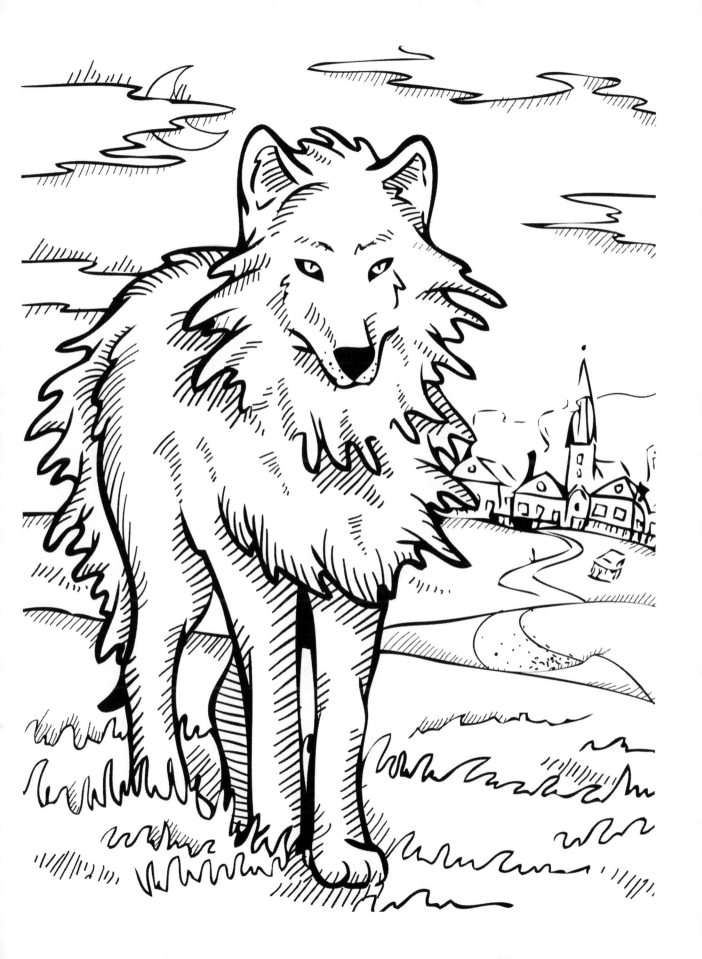

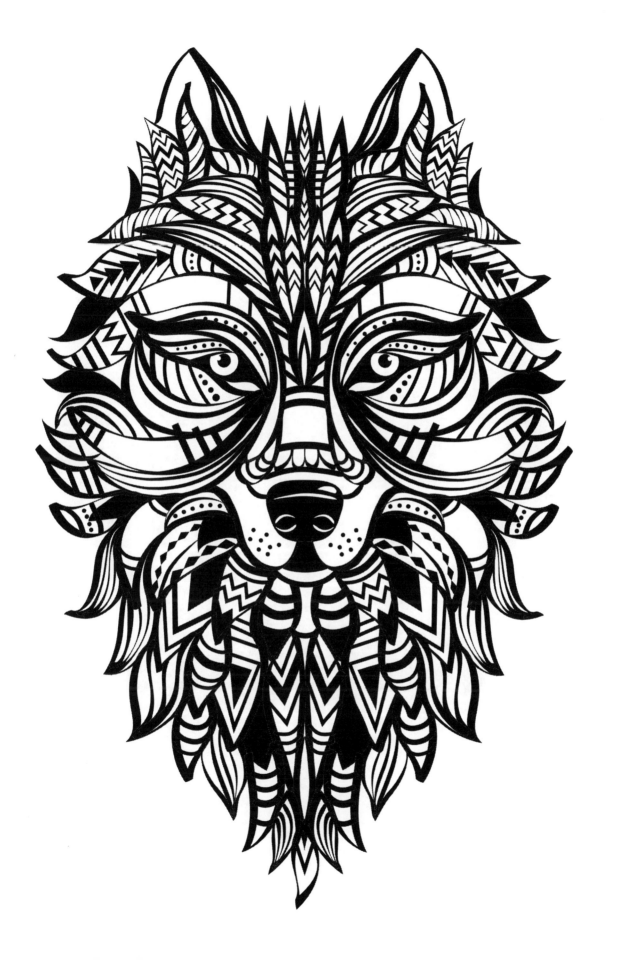

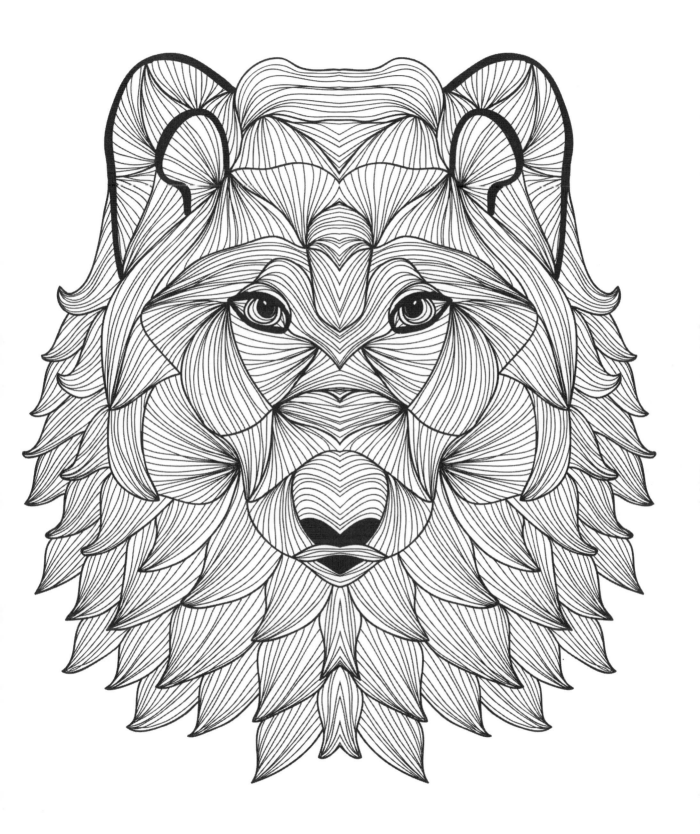

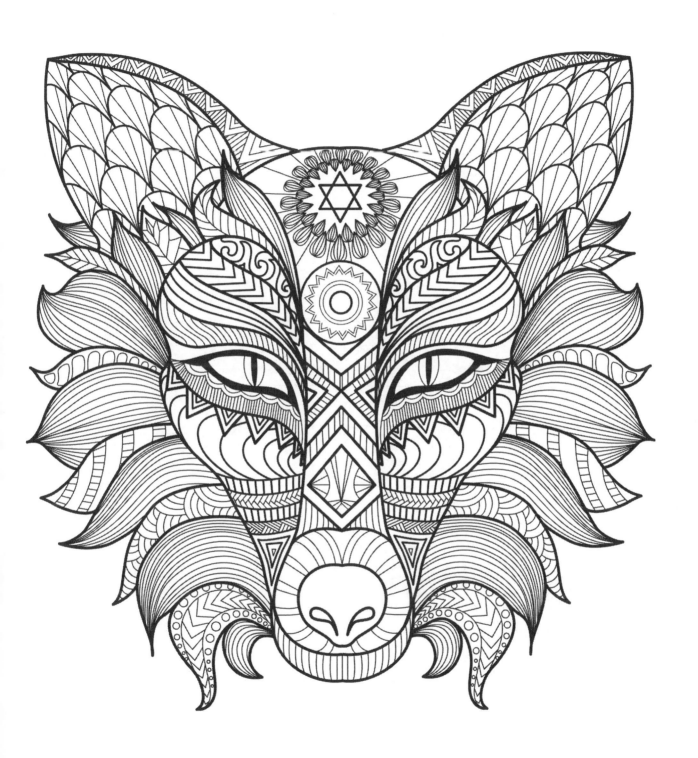

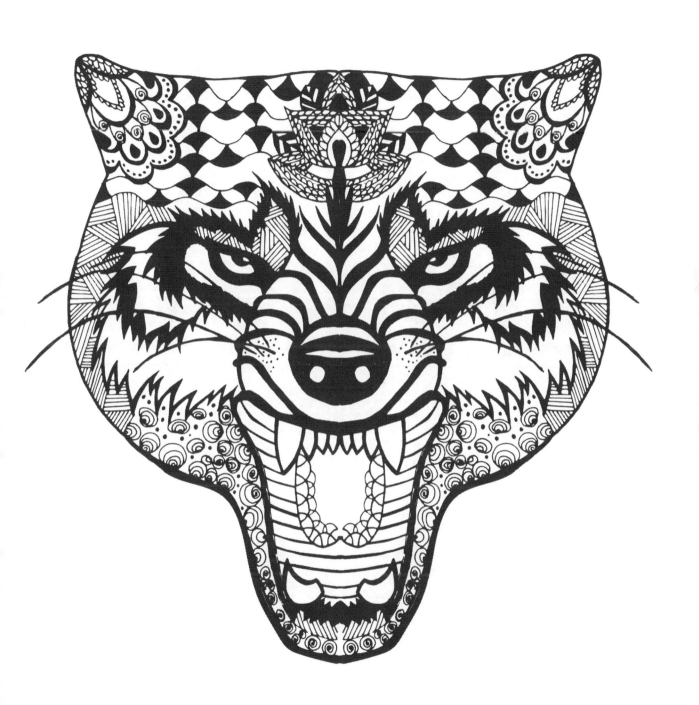

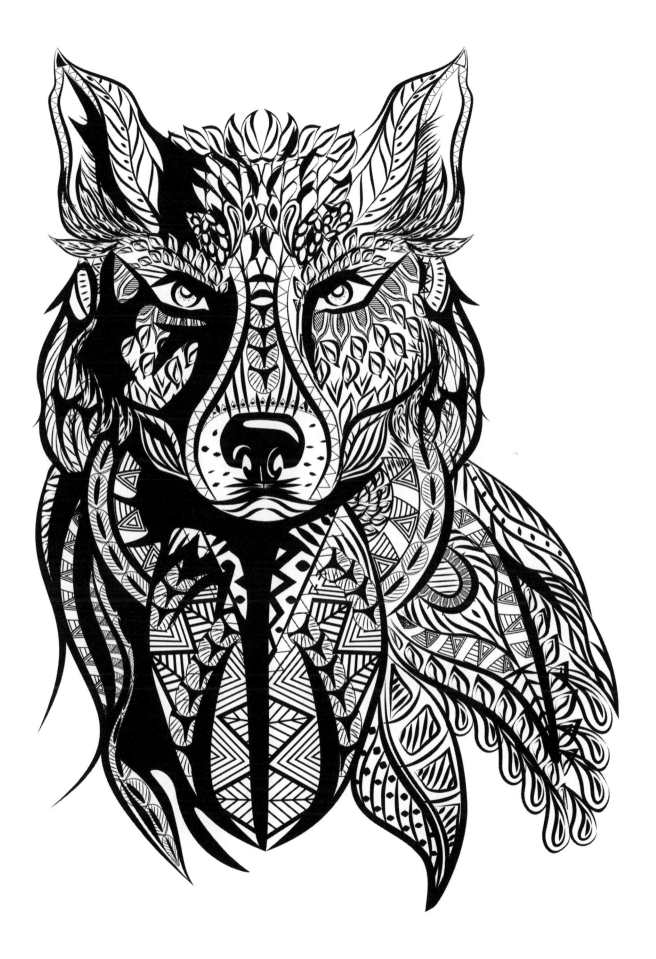

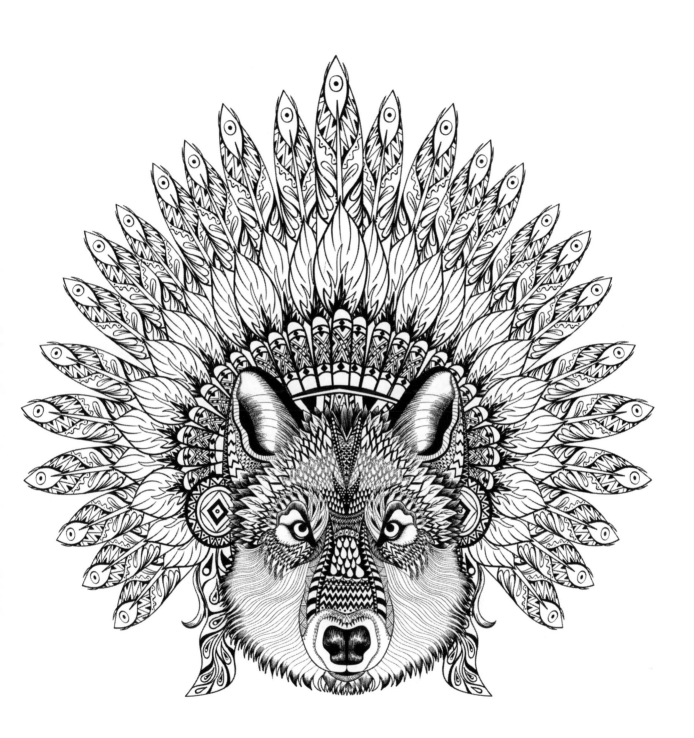

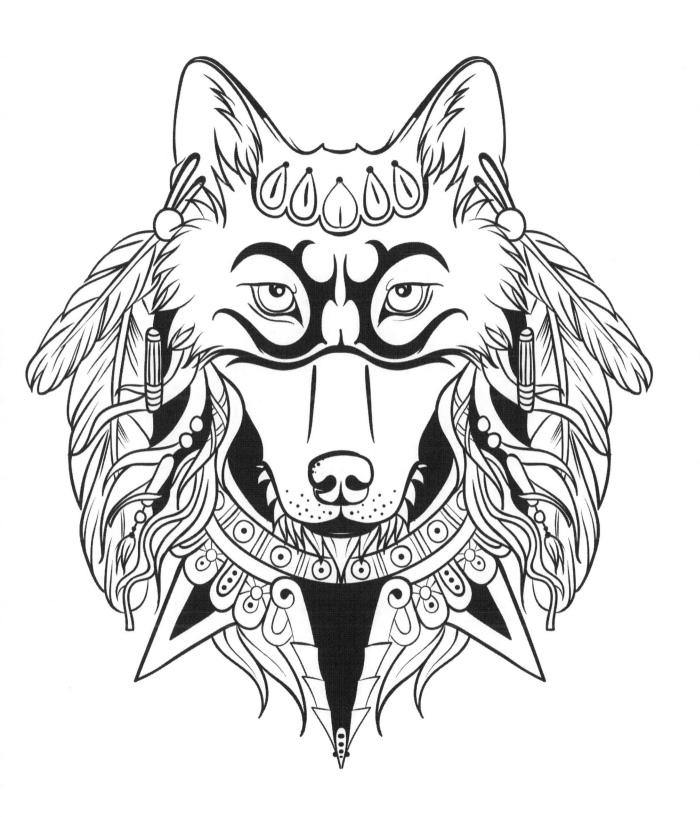

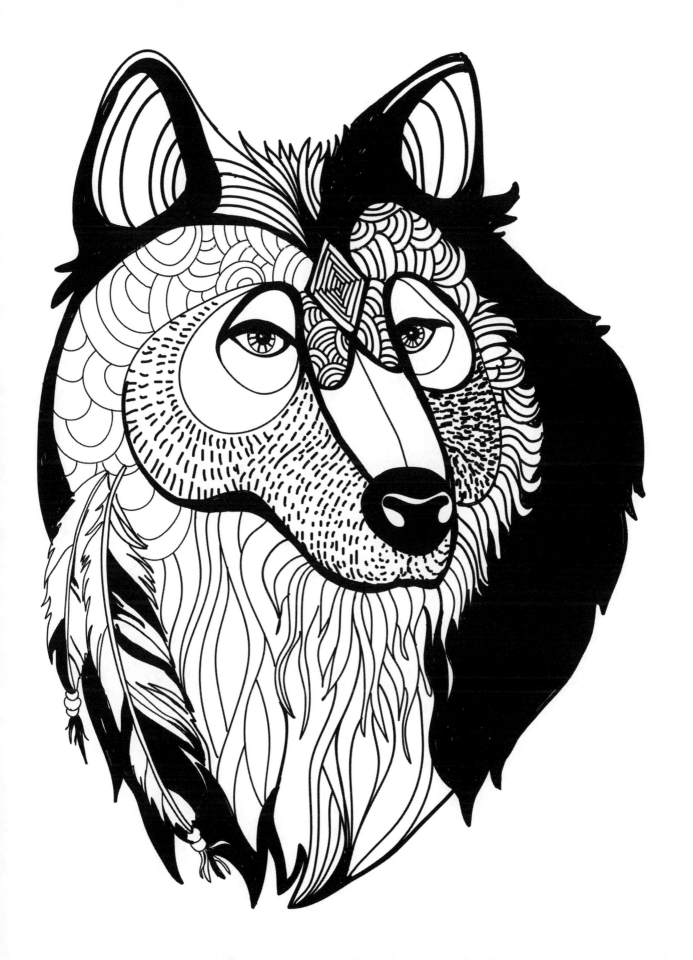

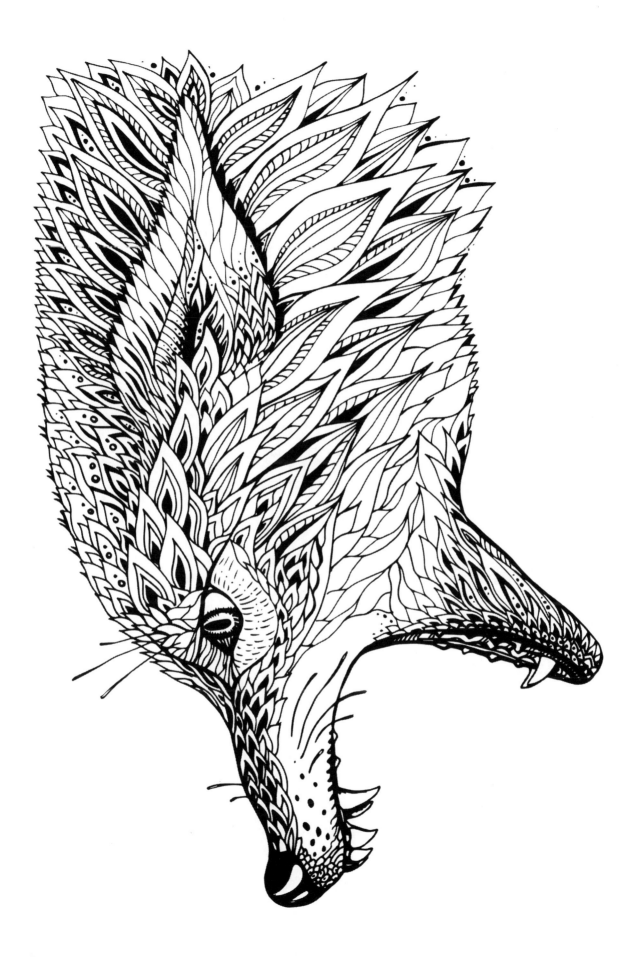

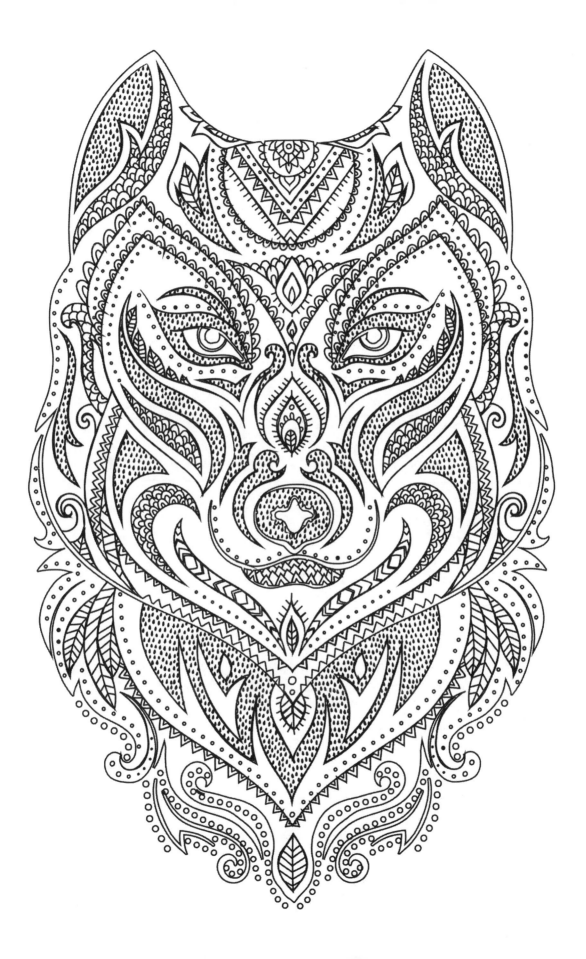

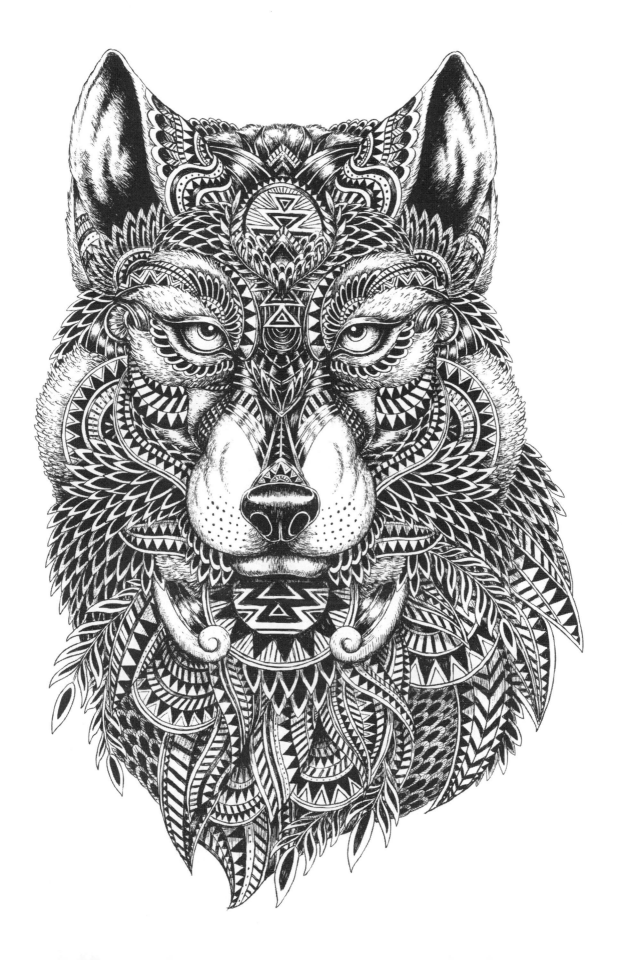

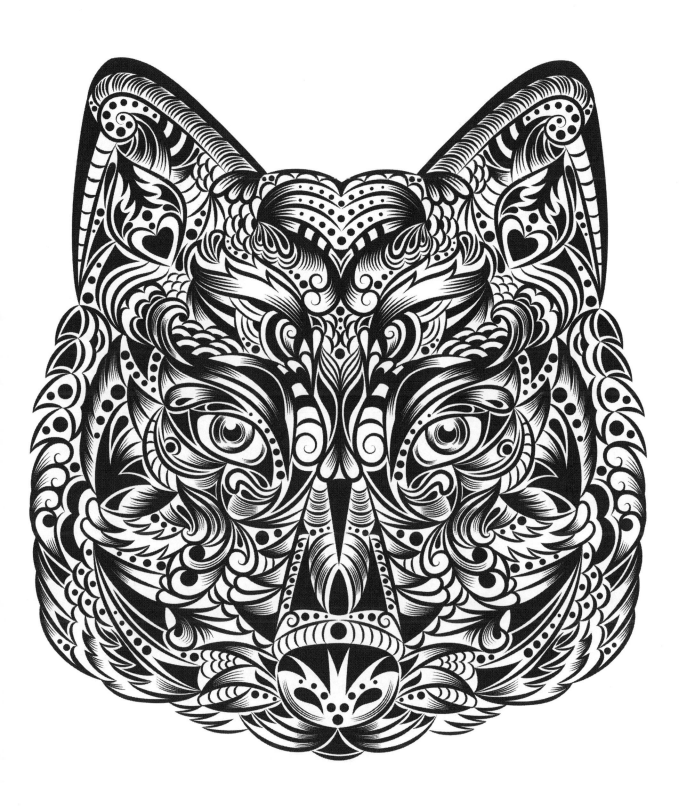

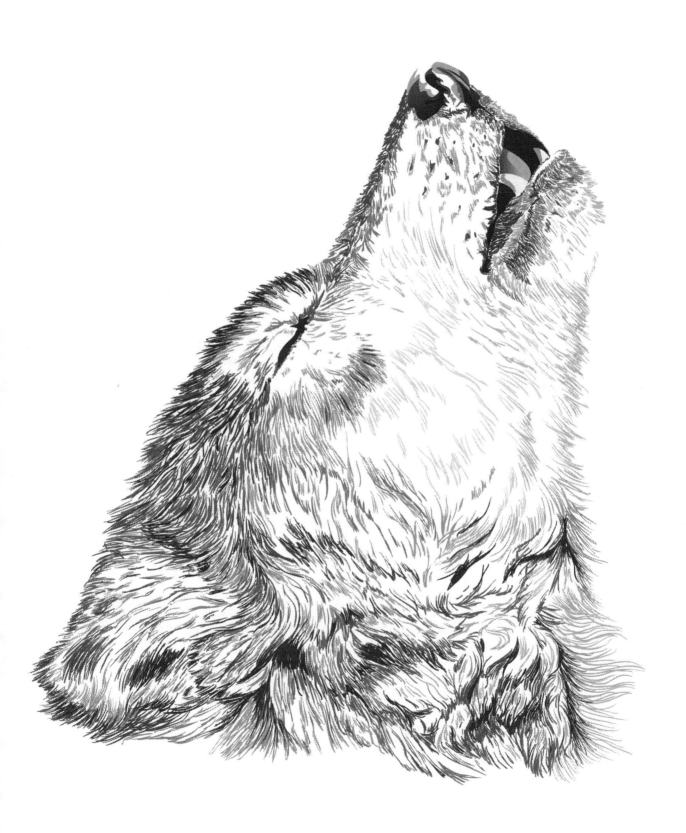

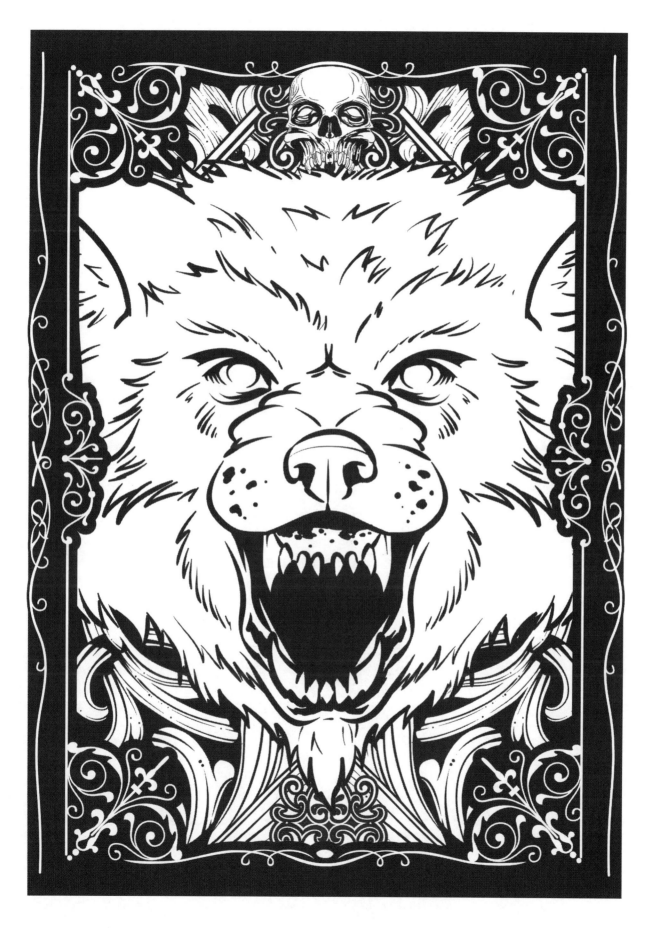

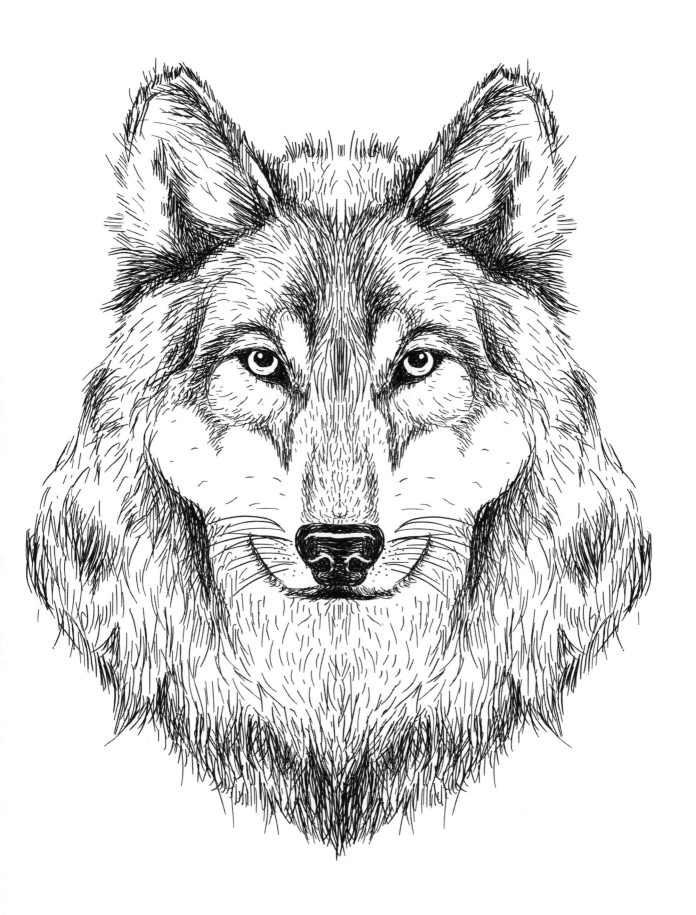

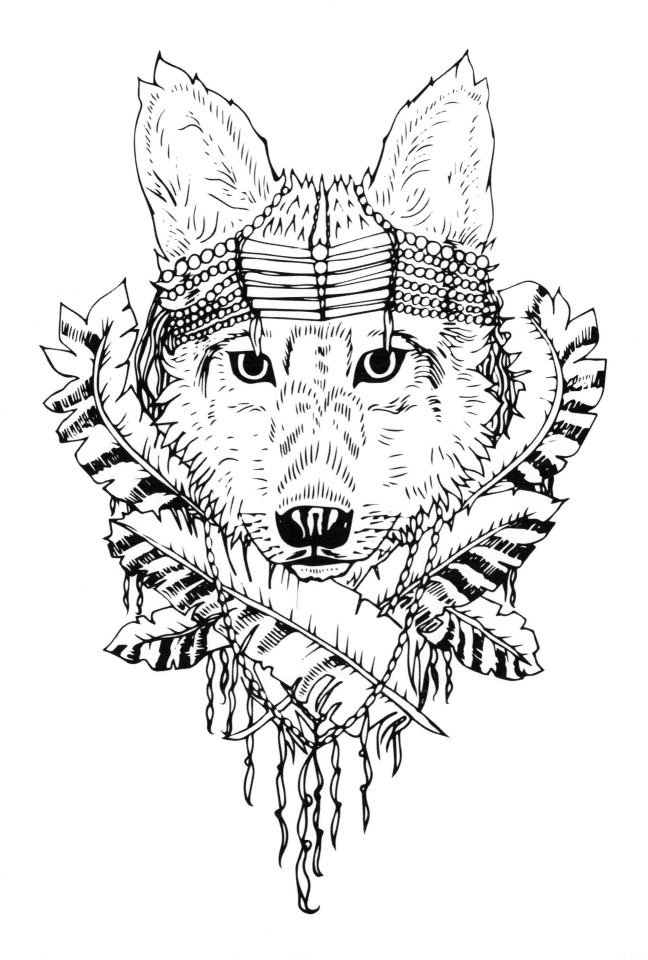

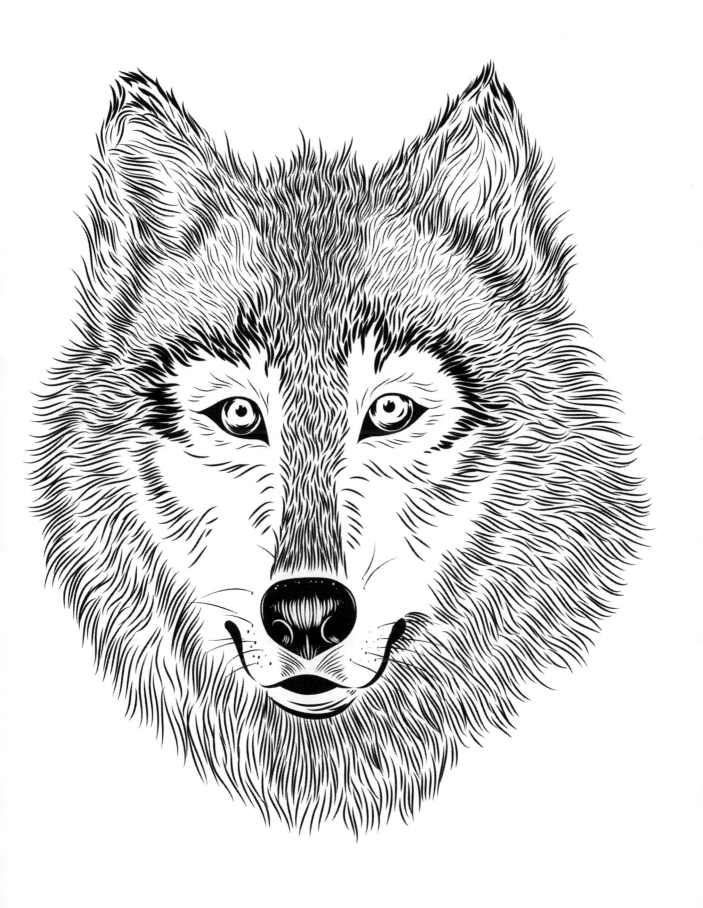

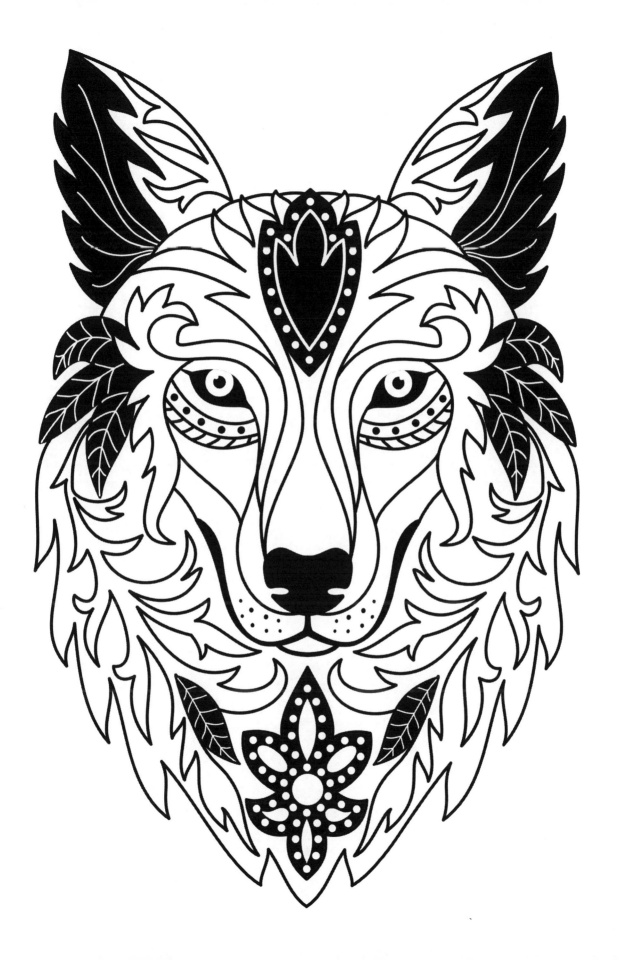

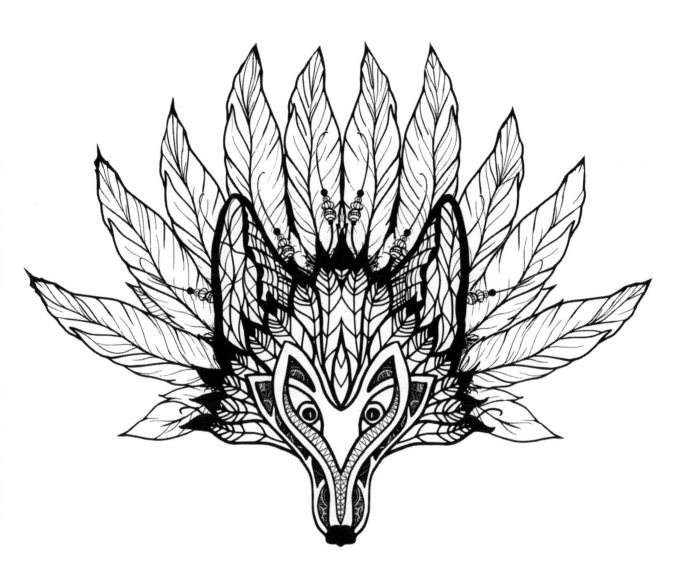

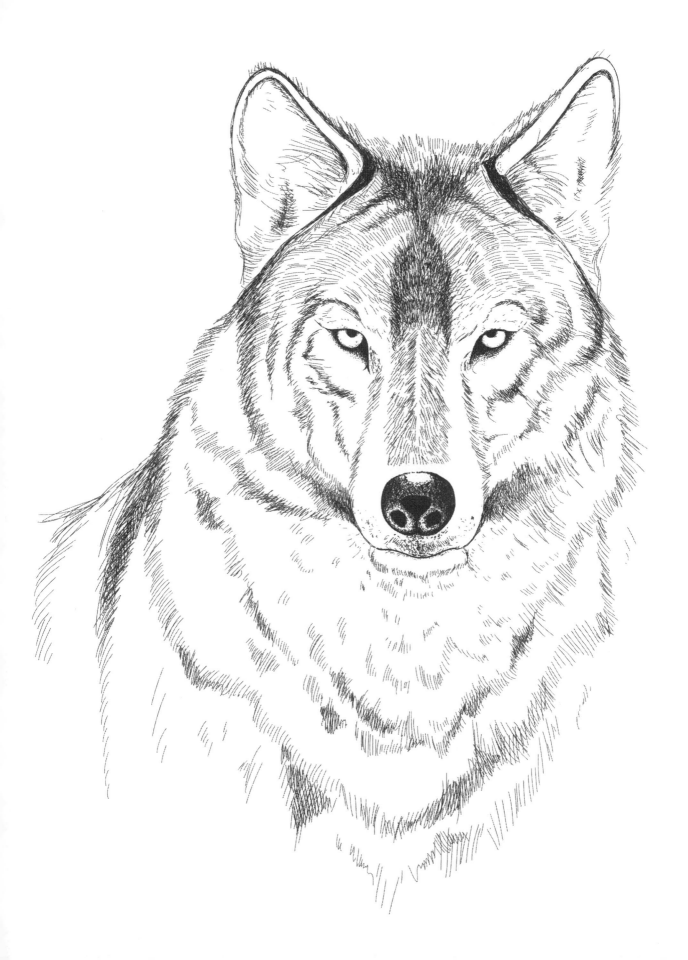

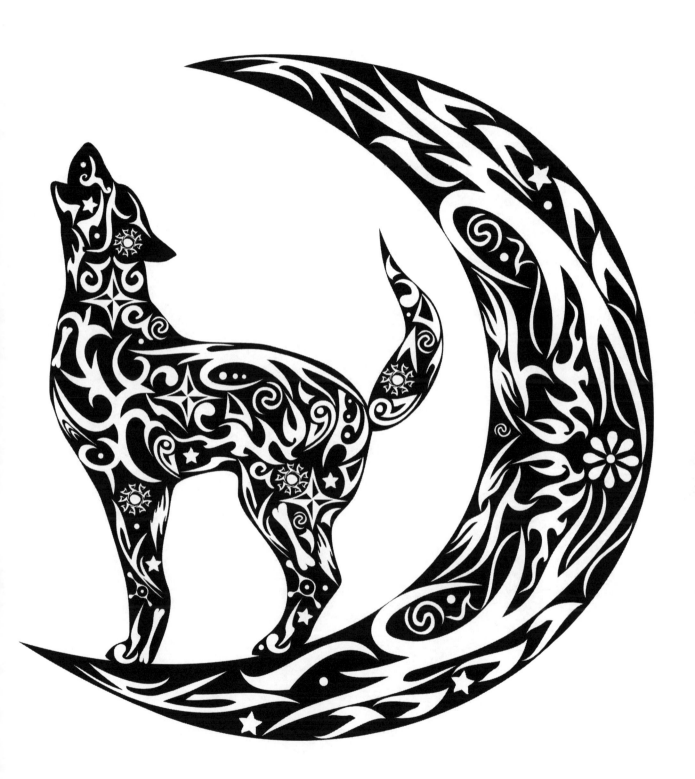

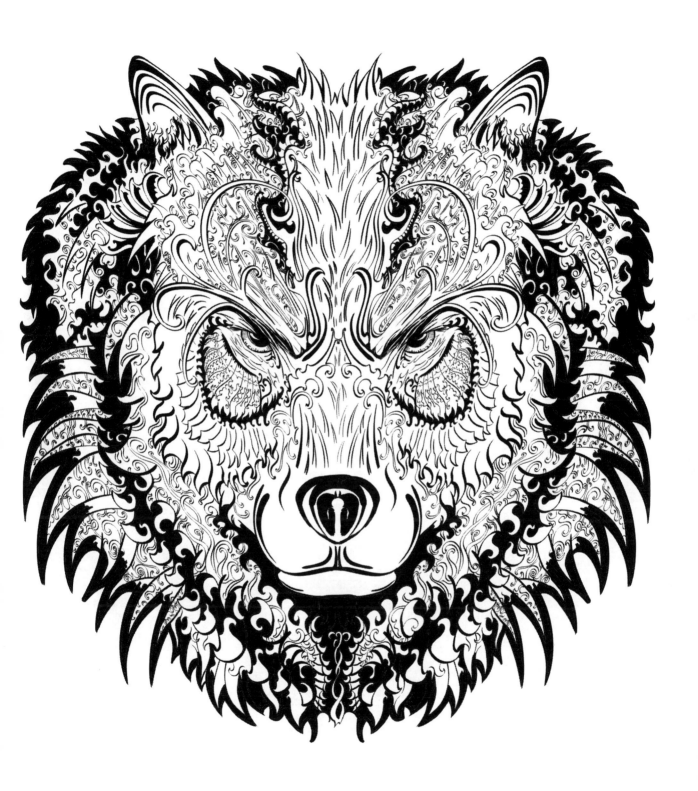

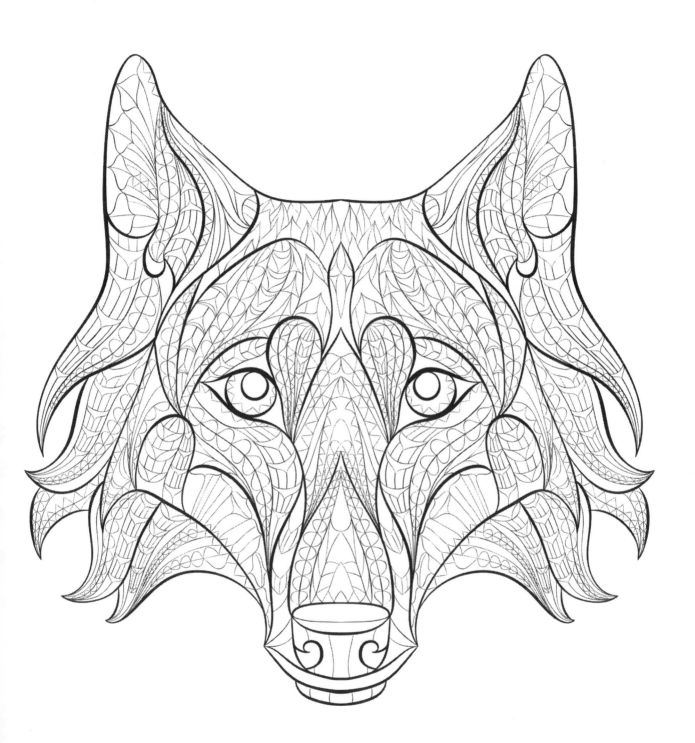

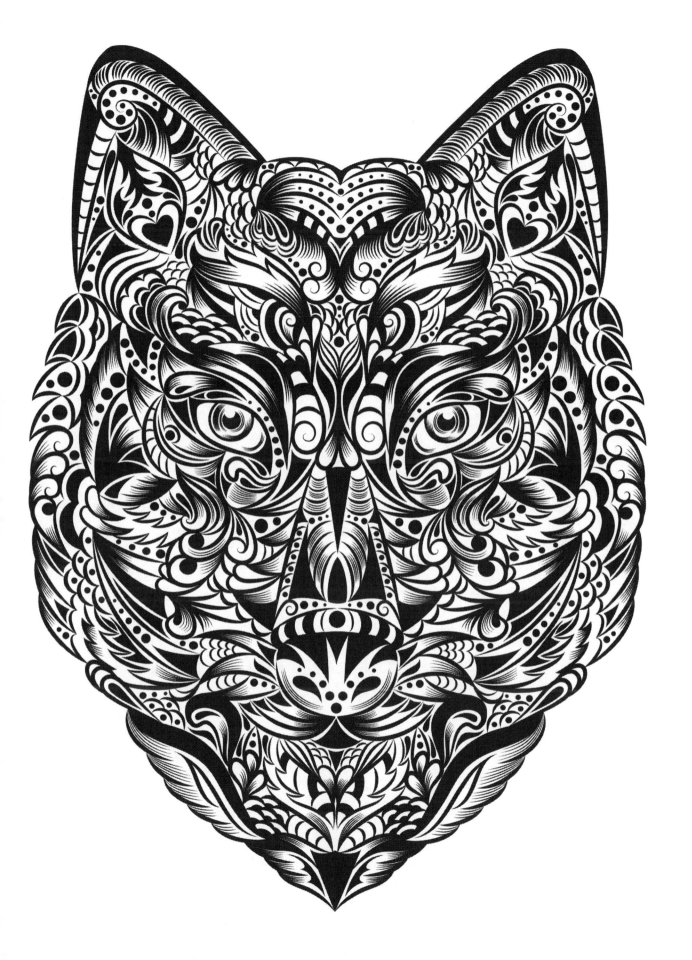

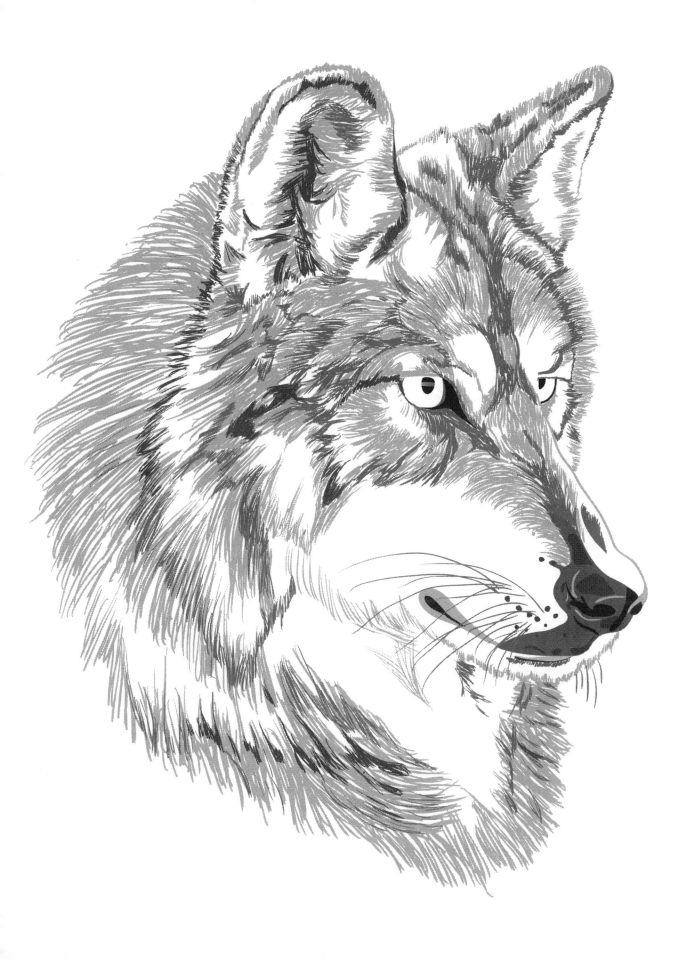

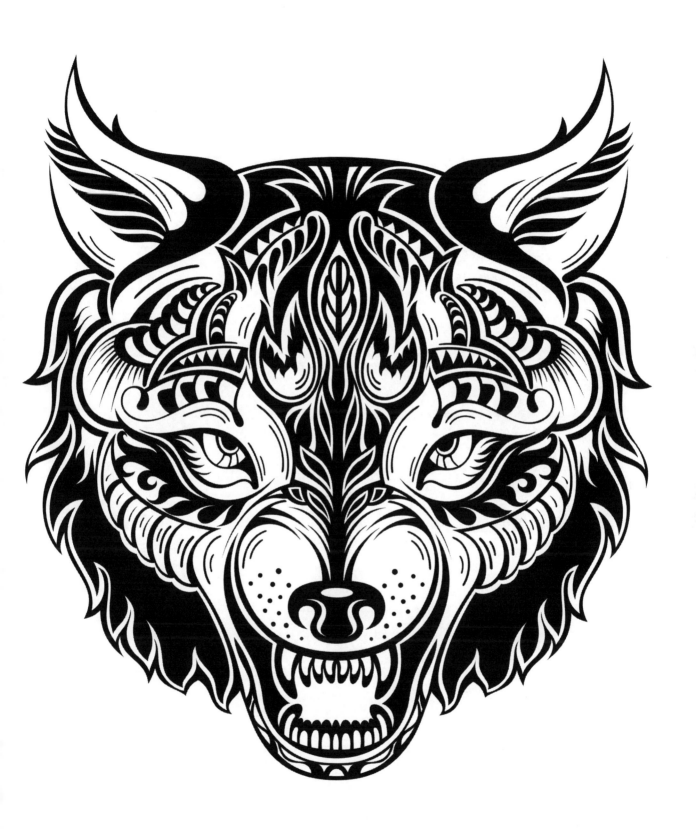

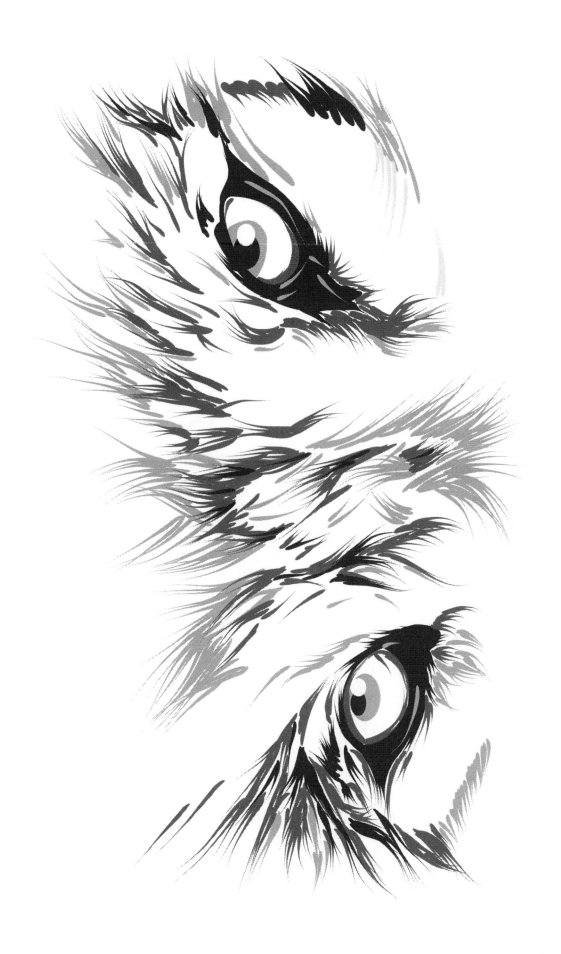

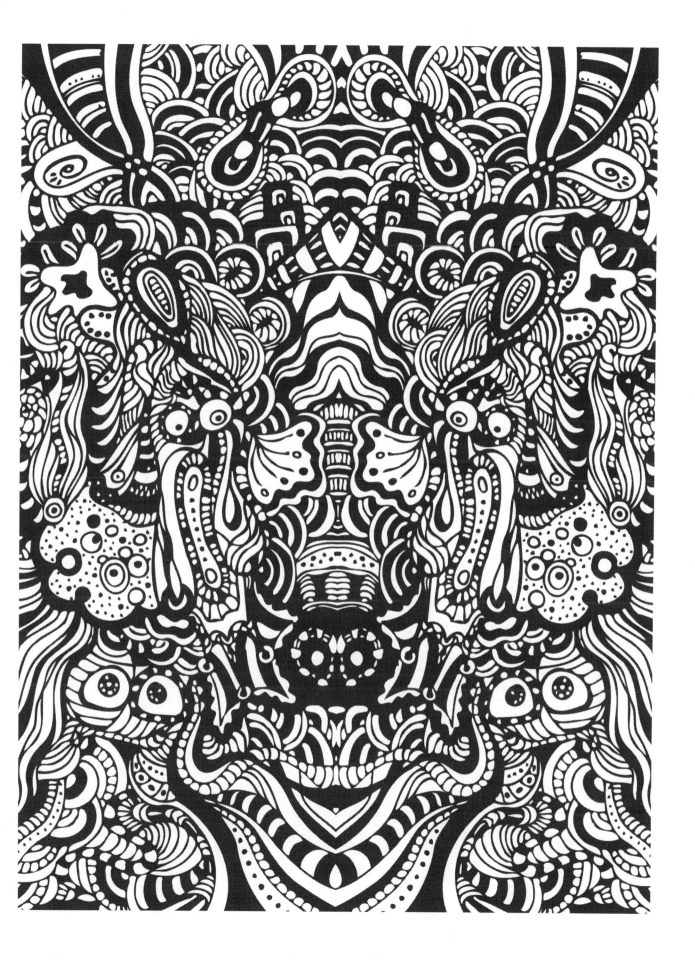

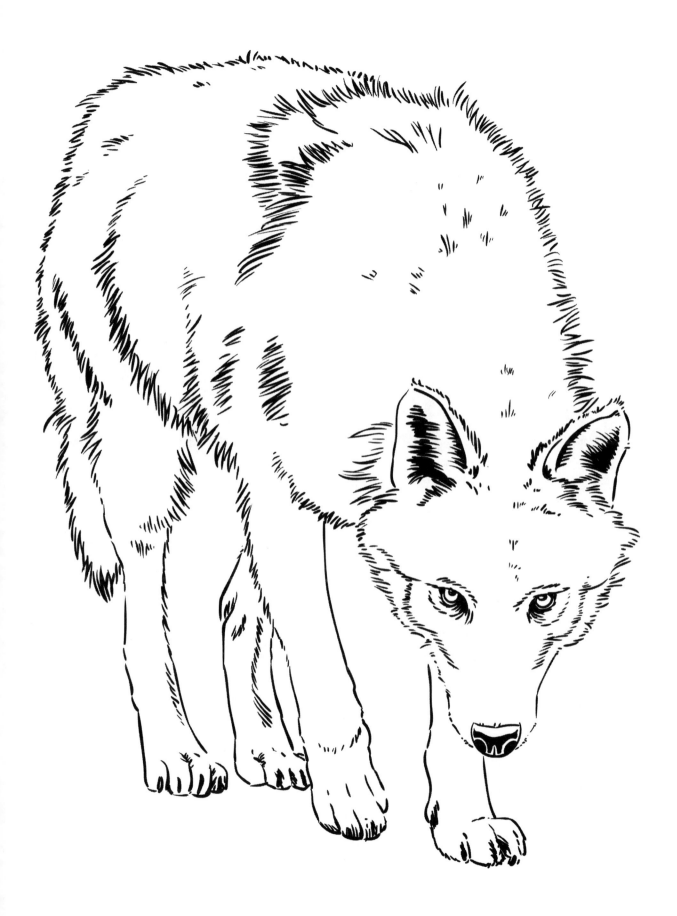

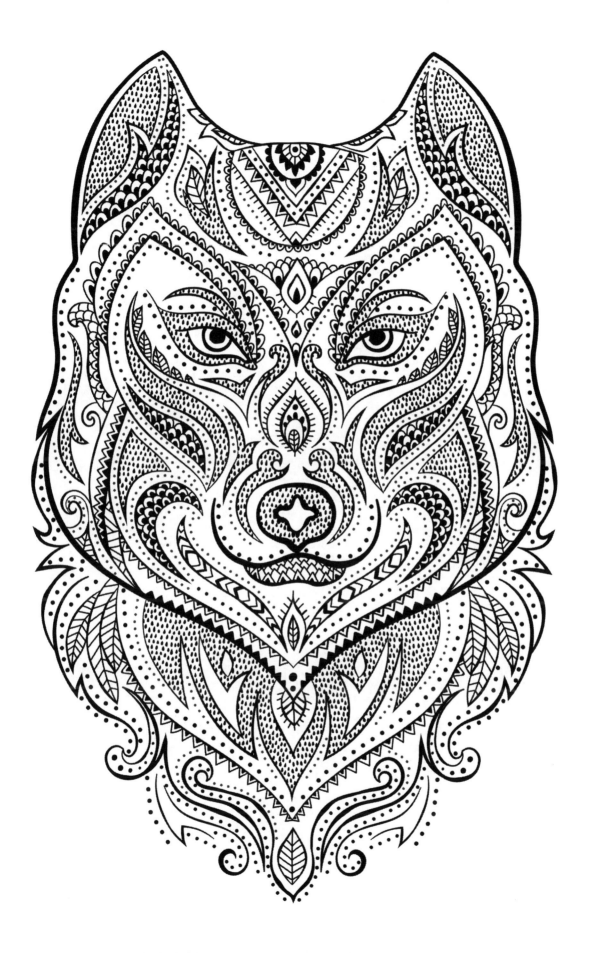

Made in the USA
San Bernardino, CA
27 November 2016